## Listen (lĭs′ən) n.
1. To apply oneself to hearing something.
2. To pay attention; give heed.

## Up (ŭp) adv.
1. From a lower to a higher position.
2. In or toward a more advanced state.
3. So as to increase or improve.

## Leader (Lē′dər) n.
1. A person who leads others along a way; a guide.

# LISTEN UP, LEADER!

## PAY ATTENTION, IMPROVE AND GUIDE

# DAVID COTTRELL
### WITH ALICE ADAMS

To order additional copies of
# Listen Up, Leader!
# Pay Attention, Improve and Guide
complete the Order Form found on the last page of this book.

For information on CornerStone Leadership
products and services
call 1-888-789-LEAD or
visit www.cornerstoneleadership.com

CornerStone
Leadership Institute*

CornerStone Leadership Institute
P.O. Box 764087
Dallas, Texas 75376
888.789.LEAD

Printed in the United States of America
ISBN: 09658788-3-x

*Book design:* Precision Type
*Cover design:* Crabtree Design

# How to Get the Most Out of This Book!

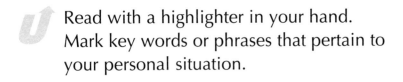 Read with a highlighter in your hand. Mark key words or phrases that pertain to your personal situation.

In the back of this book, you will find the CornerStone Principles of Leadership to serve as a guide for your leadership adventure. Refer to it frequently.

When you complete this book, order copies for those you lead so they will know that you are listening. This may encourage them to speak up as you listen up.

# CONTENTS

# INTRODUCTION

Ever wanted to know what your employees think about your leadership style? Would they say it's too demanding, too bureaucratic? Would they be willing to do more for you? Get ready for some straight answers. Read on!

Listen up! We've got something to say!

First of all, we're overachievers! Surprised? In your eyes we may look like average employees, but away from work we excel at everything!

You're our manager but you still haven't discovered what it takes to motivate us to overachieve while we're at work.

Sure, you probably think we're good people or you wouldn't have hired us. You probably think we're dependable, trustworthy and usually do the job without complaining or causing trouble. Yes, that's all true. But, we could do so much more for you and this company.

With the right signals from you, we could overachieve in our jobs the same way we overachieve in every other aspect of our lives. When it comes to our children, for example, we have a passion to help them become success-ful in life and will do whatever it takes to give them that opportunity. Our wives/husbands believe we would sacrifice everything for them — and they're right! We're involved in our churches and synagogues. We're active in little league, coach soccer, attend PTA meetings and enjoy all of the usual extracurricular activities. We love it when others depend on us to take the lead in activities that are important to us and our families.

**We could be so much more than just numbers to the company. Yet, you've never asked us to be anything more.**

Why, then, are all of us just average, everyday employees? We could be so much more than just numbers to the company. Yet, you've never asked us to be anything more. We could all be the most committed, energetic, dynamic employees you've dreamed about . . . if you would just take the time to listen.

Don't be offended. This book could have been written for any of the millions of managers who have chosen leader-ship careers. We're writing this so that you can understand how — by working together — we can all increase our job satisfaction and ultimately achieve more success.

You know, a lot of changes have occurred since we've been working together. So many of our fellow workers have left to work for other companies, we can't even recall their names now. Our turnover rate — around 30% over the past several years — seems far too high. We've heard you blame our turnover problem on "the tight job market," "Gen-Xers," and the "changing times."

Well, all of those factors may have contributed to the problem, but almost every person leaving here discovers the same problems exist in their new jobs, wherever they go. And, when we bring in a replacement, they're usually outta here in another 18 months. That just doesn't make much sense, does it?

**Keeping good people requires thought and strategies that wouldn't cost you a dime!**

Keeping good people requires thought and strategies that wouldn't cost you a dime! And we're willing to share a few of our ideas because when good people leave, we have to pick up the slack and that means more work for all of us — for the same pay.

Want to know the truth? The principle reason most people leave their jobs is because management was not meeting their needs. Get it? It is not because of pay, benefits, hours, job market, Gen-Xer values or changing times.

Our pay is competitive. Most benefit packages are generally the same, wherever you go. Work schedules are reasonable. And the job market may be good right now, but not so good that you would leave a job where you are basically happy.

And you're right. The Gen-Xers are challenging but they also have the same basic needs as the rest of the team.

You could blame senior management, but people don't usually leave a place they enjoy working and go where they do not even know the names of their new senior management team.

**You control the thermostat to the climate in which we work.**

To be candid, our peers have left because you — their immediate boss — didn't meet their needs! Yes, you have more influence over our job satisfaction than anything or anyone else. You control the thermostat to the climate in which we work.

Let's get specific. Workplace climates can be positive and motivating or negative and de-motivating, depending on the example you set as a leader. Yes, your leadership style is the single most important variable. It's the stuff separating skyrocketing success from abysmal failure.

This book is written to help you hear what we, your employees, are saying. If you really listen and then address each of these points, we assure you, we will all be better employees, we will deliver better results, turnover will decrease and you'll be a hero.

You see, our customer's satisfaction really begins with our employee's satisfaction. If our needs are not being met, we are probably not going to meet our customer's needs.

Do we want to be successful? You bet we do. That's why we show up every day. And we know you want to be successful, too. Let's work diligently to listen to each other so, together, we can make our company an extraordinary place to work.

# LISTEN UP!

## Character Matters!

**Why "LISTEN UP" about character? Today's most sought after job perk is integrity. That's right! Corporate integrity is at the top of employee "wish lists" as they look for first or new jobs. How important is it to earn employee's trust? Read on!**

Achieving short-term results does not require great leadership. Those kinds of results are easy. You can threaten us, pay us more, entice us with contests, manipulate the politics or pull some other management trick. But for us to follow you, long-term, our number one demand is that you are trustworthy. Yes, even more important than having a great vision, being a great communicator or being innovative, wise, courageous, inspiring, intelligent or any other trait you can name. The first question every person on our team asks is, "Do I trust my manager and the people I work for?"

If the answer is no, then we start looking for someone else to follow, someone who we *can* trust. This trust issue is a big deal because it is a by-product of your integrity.

[ 5 ]

Without integrity, you can never develop trust. Without trust, you will never develop people. Without developing people, you will never maintain a following and without followers, you have no one to lead. See, it all begins with your integrity.

Oh, we know what you're thinking: "This is too easy. If I have anything, it's integrity." Well, you may be right, but there is a gap between what you think integrity is and what we employees judge your integrity to be.

In fact, if you asked all of us for our definitions of integrity, you would get a smorgasbord of answers. In our day-to-day experiences, integrity is questioned so frequently many of us have become callused. In some of our meetings, we have discussed unbelievable integrity issues we see in the newspaper almost every day. For 18 months, we talked about our president and how could he lie when he knew the truth would eventually be exposed. In Dallas, the superintendent of schools embezzled $16,000 worth of furniture and lost her $200,000-a-year job. We all agreed it was almost unbelievable for her to risk everything she had worked for all of her life, all for a mere $16,000!

In one of our weekly meetings, you mentioned the City of Miami had 33% of their workers on workers compensation or disability. You laughed when you shared that seven of the workers were out because of paper cuts, of all things. So, we have talked a lot about the integrity of others, but you have never asked how we judge your integrity. Isn't that strange?

The most important requirement for any manager is integrity — and we've never had that discussion!

Since we're discussing it now, we'll tell you how we judge your integrity. We do not judge it by major mistakes, like the ones in the newspapers. But we *do* judge your integrity by what we see every day.

When you criticize one of our fellow employees in public, you lose our trust. When you encourage us to stretch the truth to get an order and "we will deal with it later," your integrity is questioned. When you show favoritism, choose not to return phone calls, say you are out of the office when you really are there, or say that you didn't receive a message when you did — all these instances take a toll on our trust in you. As your followers, our integrity questions to you are these:

> The most important requirement for any manager is integrity.

- "When is a lie small enough that it does not matter?"

- "Is there a point that the small lies are okay and the big lies are not?"

- "Where is that point and how do we know when we cross the line?"

And here is the answer: There are no lies so small that it doesn't matter — and when you sacrifice your integrity, you lose your most precious leadership possession. Losing your integrity is kind of like boiling a frog.

Okay, you may need this explanation if you've never boiled a frog before: When you put a frog in boiling water, almost immediately that frog will realize that he is in danger and will jump out to get away from that boiling pot. But, put that same frog in a pot of cold water on a stove and gradually increase the temperature until it boils, and he will remain in the pot, unaware of the subtle temperature changes until he, quite literally, boils to death.

Make sense? Well, this is how you lose your integrity with your team . . . one degree of dishonesty at a time. You see, there are no varying degrees of integrity. We make the judgement if you have integrity or not based on what we see. You're probably not even aware when you've lost our trust, maybe because you've become immune to the minor lies — which have become a major problem for all of us.

As minor as those lies may seem, just remember that we do not forget your integrity mistakes. We will forget and forgive any judgement error that you make, but integrity mistakes are forever.

**We will forget and forgive any judgement error that you make, but integrity mistakes are forever.**

So how you can earn our trust and protect your most precious leadership tool?

First, we have to understand your vision of success. The more clearly we understand your vision the more effective we will be in helping you achieve that vision. Answer these questions for us:

- What is our purpose in that vision?
- What are the values that you will not compromise for any reason?

- What code of behavior is acceptable to fulfill that purpose?
- What are your goals that will ensure we accomplish your vision?

Once we understand those elements, you can then establish a common mission that we all will help you achieve.

The connection between your vision of success and your integrity is what you do. We know that you are not perfect but we want you to do these four things:

1. **Keep your promises.** You don't have to promise things just to make us feel good. We are more interested in being able to depend on what you promise than we are interested in feeling good. Just keep the promises you do make to us and we'll trust what you say.

2. **Stand up and speak out for what you think is important.** We cannot read your mind. We do not know how you feel. If we are guessing how you feel about something, we'll probably guess wrong. Save us the trouble. Tell us how you feel and why. We will respect you so much more.

3. **Err on the side of fairness.** Be fair to all of us. We know things are not always clearly right or wrong. Sometimes you have to make difficult decisions that affect many people. Sometimes these decisions include having to de-hire some of us. All we ask is that you are fair at all times, regardless of the type of decisions you have to make.

4.  **Do what you say you are going to do.** Just let your "yes" be "yes" and your "no" mean "no." When you tell us you're going to do something, we should "consider it done."

Are you surprised that we would put integrity this high on our list of priorities? Most leaders think their followers put vision or communication or problem-solving skills first. Of course, all of those attributes are important, but what difference do they make if we do not trust you? Does it matter what vision you provide if we cannot trust that your vision is best for all of us? Does it matter how well you communicate if we can't trust what you say? Does it matter how charismatic you are if you have no one willing to follow?

**Integrity=Trust=People Development=Followers=Leadership**

See, it all starts with your integrity. We want you to be successful and we want to be successful, but we will follow you only after you have earned our trust!

# LISTEN UP!

## We don't want to hear excuses!

**Why "LISTEN UP" about accountability?** Whether you like it or not, the buck stops with you. When a glitch occurs, no one has time for excuses. Taking responsibility is the name of the game – and tag, you're it!

Each one of us is an important part of your team.

Even though we work for a large company, you are our leader. We don't follow the company's mission statement, senior management memos, annual reports, or what the stock market watchers say about us. We follow you . . . and, like it or not, you are not only our leader but also a large part of our career success. Our job happiness depends on our relationship.

Don't take this lightly. Sometimes we lie awake nights, worried about you and how you feel about things. We could be wondering why you passed one of us in the hall without even acknowledging that we existed. We could be

[ 11 ]

wondering why you took some of us behind closed doors and left others behind.  As our leader, you are important—to all of us!

If anyone told you leadership was easy, they lied.  We watch every day, seeing you assume incredible responsibilities.  You are responsible for your actions and for our actions, plus all the fiscal requirements, employee problems, feedback, training, embracing technology, hiring, de-hiring, communicating, staff development, prioritizing, eliminating unnecessary bureaucracy and much more.  Your job is tough but it's the job you chose.

What we ask of you is to accept responsibility for being the very best at your job so we can be the best at our jobs.

When you became our manager, the game changed.

Everything you do is exaggerated . . . watched under a magnifying glass.

You're now held to a higher level of accountability than before.  In fact, everything you do is exaggerated . . . watched under a magnifying glass.  And, when you're down, we're down.  When you're up, we're up. You set the tone . . . you create the environment in which we can be successful.

Because of this, we expect more from you than anyone else in the entire company and we want you to lead us without excuses.

When you accepted all the responsibilities of leadership, you lost some of your rights.  That's right.  You lost the right to be cynical, negative, to blame others, to be a member of our "pity parties" and even the right to some of your private time. Everything that happens in our workgroup is now your personal responsibility.

One of the most stressful situations you can experience is when you feel that you are out of control. The faster you realize that you control everything that impacts our workgroup, the sooner you can eliminate stress by taking total responsibility and getting on with helping us be successful.

There are a couple of truths of leadership that you need to know. **First, we are watching everything you do.** Even when you think we're not paying attention, we are. There is never a time when you are not leading. You may think that because you choose to ignore an issue, you are not leading. You are wrong! When you consistently show up late for meetings, you lead us to believe our time is not important. When you  lose your cool and over-react over small details, we wonder how you would react when something big comes along. It's a fact. You are always leading. You can never not lead!

**Secondly, everything you do counts.** Sometimes, you may want to share juicy gossip and remove yourself from your leadership role. Don't be fooled. You can not let go of your leadership role that easily. Everything counts! It is like being on a diet and eating salad all day. Then when you go home, you reward yourself with two pieces of cheesecake because you have been so good all day. After polishing off the last bite, you try to convince yourself that

the cheesecake does not matter. Then you weigh yourself
. . . obviously, it does matter! The same is true about your
leadership. Even though you have been a "professional"
all day, don't think that what you say to us away from the
office doesn't count. Everything counts.

And, we don't want to hear any excuses . . . about
anything. But, if you're committed to be a great leader,
and you want us to be committed followers there are three
things we will demand:

**Hire great people.** We want people on our team
who have a desire to be here, a talent for doing the
job, and whose values fit with our corporate values.
Finding and hiring the right people is
the most important thing you do.
Take your time. Involve us in the
process — and let's get people who
will help us be successful. Let's face
facts! You can be the greatest
manager in the world but if you have
people who are not talented on our
team, we will not be successful. We all want to be
surrounded with talented people who have skills
and talents to contribute to our success. Don't let us
down and hire a "warm body," just to fill a position.
When you do this, it becomes a lot more work for
all of us!

> Finding and hiring the right people is the most important thing you do.

**De-hire the people on our team who are not
contributing to our mission.** We know that letting
someone go is not easy. We're glad we don't have
this responsibility. But, look around. Some of the

people on our team are killing us! In fact, they're more detrimental to our success than any of our competitors.

We've seen you ignore the problem, work around the problem and joke about the problem. You have coached them and done everything you can do. It looks like you spend more time cleaning up after them than recognizing our achievements. So, get on with it! We're depending on you to provide the best atmosphere for us to be successful and, unfortunately, it's your responsibility to deal with the problem employees. Be fair, but let them go to work somewhere else. If we get lucky maybe they will find a job with one of our competitors.

> ... it's your responsibility to deal with the problem employees. Be fair, but let them go to work somewhere else.

**Treat us with respect.** Our deepest needs are to be understood and treated with respect and dignity. One of the common questions around here is, "Why are the managers such an elitist group?"

The old Golden Rule should be your Number One Rule. Just treat us like you would want to be treated if you were in our jobs. Sure, your paycheck may be more than our paycheck but, collectively, you need us more than we need you.

Don't get us wrong. We're not minimizing the importance of what you do, but if you were to lose all of us, it would impact the company a whole lot more than if we were to lose you.

So, treat us with dignity and respect and be sensitive to our needs.

Your leadership and the decisions you make contribute more to our success than all other factors combined. We depend on you to accept responsibility for all you control — and you control the destiny of our team.

If you surround us with talented people, we will be an excellent organization. If you want us to be a strong and effective organization, surround us with strong and effective people.

**If you want us to be a strong and effective organization, surround us with strong and effective people.**

If you choose to accept total responsibility – and no excuses for failure, we will help you achieve more success than you ever imagined possible.

# LISTEN UP!

## We want to know
## where we are headed.

One of the main reasons people leave our company is because they're confused about the direction we're going.

It's probably hard to see from your position, but there's not a lot of clarity, not a lot of direction in what we're supposed to be doing. In fact, the mission statement hanging on the wall says one thing, you tell us another and our compensation rewards us for something else.

On top of that, our job descriptions were written four years ago – in another time for another purpose — and when performance reviews come around, you tell us we should have been doing something completely different.

No wonder we are confused!

Whether you believe it or not, each person on our team wastes close to 5.5 hours a week because of unclear communication about where we are going. That's seven weeks per year — per person!

> Each person on our team wastes close to 5.5 hours a week because of unclear communication about where we are going.

If you want to achieve better results and improve our morale, clearly communicate where we are going — and why.

We've all talked about this before and we've decided there's a secret to retaining good employees and getting better results. It's a recipe with four important ingredients:

**Ingredient One: We want to know your vision - what you want us to accomplish.** The corporate vision is great for the annual report but your vision is what we need to see. Your vision should be a clear understanding of what our team's results could be and how you want this to happen. Help us want to follow your lead. Figure out exactly what you want us to accomplish and we'll help you develop a plan to get it done.

We are not good at guessing what your vision is, so just tell us and give us a chance to make it happen. The number one stress we experience happens when we do not know what is expected – of each of us. Oh yes, we know . . . you give job descriptions and performance reviews, but we still are not sure exactly what you expect. When you depend on our perceptions to meet your expectations, you are going to be disappointed every time.

> When you depend on our perceptions to meet your expectations, you are going to be disappointed every time.

The "disconnect" between us — leader and followers — is consistency. When you tell us one thing and reward us for another thing, we get confused. This inconsistency creates stress and, frankly, most of us don't work well under that type of stress. When we do not know your expectations, we get sidetracked – lost, afraid, doubting — and an internal conflict develops. Just tell us what you want and we will do what you need.

**Ingredient Two: We want to know how you think we are doing.** Please do not assume we all know how you think we're doing because if we were not doing well you would let us know. We need to hear from you – whether we're doing it right or wrong! You're not around every time we do a good job so you cannot always tell us. You may think you wear yourself out, telling us how we are doing, but we are all insecure to a certain degree. We need to hear positive recognition from you. When you see something you like, tell us. We need to know that we are "okay" in your eyes.

**Ingredient Three: We want to know that you care.** This question, "does anybody really give a flip around here," comes up almost daily. Recently we asked each other –

over coffee — what really motivates each of us to go above and beyond the normal job description. Number one on the list was that we wanted to be appreciated by you, our immediate manager – and our leader.

Yes, it came in above money, interesting work and promotions! Number two was to be in the planning stages of things at work, not just implement decisions other people make. Number three was that we wanted to work for a boss who was empathetic when any of us had a problem. Then came money — fourth on the list. A paycheck doesn't show that leadership cares. Everyone earns a paycheck. What shows us you care is when you spend time with us, listen to us and have a genuine interest in how we are, personally as well as professionally. If you do not show us you care, we assume that you don't. Then, we begin not to care, either.

> **If you do not show us you care, we assume that you don't. Then, we begin not to care, either.**

**Ingredient Four: We want to know how our team is doing and where we fit into the bigger picture.** We all feel like winners — most of the time — but sometimes we don't know if we are winning or losing because we don't know how the score is being calculated.

Our competitive nature is to win and contribute to something greater and bigger than just our workgroup. Give us that opportunity. Show us how you're keeping score and help us learn how to keep score, too. Reward us for winning, help us regroup when we fall down and we will be able to reach higher than you ever imagined!

The secret of retention really boils down to communication and building trust. E-mails, voice-mails, and memos are all effective methods of communication but they do not develop trust. Honestly, we don't think you can develop trust electronically. Trust happens only when there is consistent, personal communication — and caring.

> **The secret of retention really boils down to communication and building trust.**

You may get the results you're trying to accomplish without a clearly defined vision. You may get those same results, whether or not you let us how we are doing. You may not take the time to let us know you care and you may not think it's important to keep us informed about our team's results. But, this is for sure — there will turnover, poor morale and you will be settling for less than our full potential all along the way.

We want to help. Just give us the chance.

# LISTEN UP!

## What you reward gets done!

Do you ever wonder why we sometimes don't do what you want? You want us to do a good job and we want to do a good job. It's not rocket science – so why do we sometimes disappoint each other with our results? Read on!

One of the primary principles of leadership is that you get what you reward. Sound familiar? Does Pavlov ring a bell?

In the past this principle has worked against our success as much as it has helped. It may sound strange but sometimes the things that are being rewarded around here are not really what you want to happen. In fact, many times the opposite of what you want is the behavior that's rewarded. Doesn't make good sense, does it?

Let me explain because our team is a perfect example. We all know everyone on our team does not contribute at the same level.  Our team performance could be broken down into three groups.  About 30% of our team members are top performers — people who will do whatever it takes to get the job done.  We also have people on our team who have the talent to do what needs to be done but chose not to do it all the time.  This group represents about 50% of our team.  Then there are the other 20% — team members who make no contribution much of the time and actually hinder us from achieving certain goals.  You have probably identified each of the groups while reading this paragraph.

So what happens when you have a special project that comes along with a quick deadline?  You do not burden the bottom 20% of our team with the project, do you? You do not even involve the middle 50% of our team in the project.  No, it's usually the top 30% you "reward" with extra work every time.

The people you depend on most are the ones you trust, but they are also the ones who get most of the work.  We don't blame you for depending on the top performers.  And sometimes the additional work is really okay because high performers are usually the team members wanting to learn and grow.  But many times, your confidence in the superstars just means more work with no reward.  This drives people crazy!

Many times your confidence in the superstars just means more work with no reward. This drives people crazy!

When this becomes a constant pattern, we have seen some of our top performers begin figuring out how to move into the middle group where they do not have to do the additional work. The middle group then tries to figure out how to get into the lower group where even less is required. Obviously the performance of our whole team suffers. Then we all wonder, "What is the problem?"

Why not just hold everybody accountable for his or her performance?

If there is not positive "reward" for superb performance, common sense will tell you that superb performance will not continue. I have even heard several of my peers say that they choose not to do some of your more demanding assignments. When we are actually punished with additional work for doing what you want, we will find a way to avoid that punishment. Our sales people say the same thing. They say that the best sales people are rewarded with higher and higher sales quotas until they are forced to become "average" performers. That just doesn't make sense to any of us.

It is not our job to tell you to discipline team members for not performing but you should know that you are penalizing your best people when you choose to ignore those who refuse to do their jobs.

When all is said and done, there are only a few reasons why your team does not do what you want us to do:

> You are penalizing your best people when you choose to ignore those who refuse to do their jobs.

**We are not sure what you want us to do.** When you continually change our mission without ever telling us, we probably are not going to do what you want us to do. It is not that we don't care — it's that there is so much ambiguity that we cannot understand where our focus should be. We will do what you want us to do if we clearly understand what it is and why it is important.

**We don't know how to do it.** Yes, training, is a big issue around here. Most of us are in our jobs because we were the best at our previous jobs. That's no guarantee that we will be successful at our new positions — without training. Please, do not take for granted that we know how to do everything in our job description. Train us how you want things done, give us the tools and we will deliver the results.

Give us the tools and we will deliver the results.

**Your reward system is not aligned with our group goals.** When we are rewarded for doing a good job and punished when we do not do a good job, we will do what you want us to do. Don't punish us for being star performers.

**Sometimes you wont' let us do what we need to do.** I know this is hard for you to believe but it is true. When we are called into unnecessary meetings, we can't do what we need to do to achieve our goals. When you interrupt us several times a day, we are not going to be as productive as we can be. When you ignore our requests for support, we are not able to get things done as efficiently as we should. You see, even though you're not aware of what is keeping us from doing what we need to do, sometimes it's because you are preventing us from doing our job.

What you reward is what you will receive. Keep that in mind the next time you are trying to figure out why you're not getting the results you expect.

# LISTEN UP!

## Don't be afraid to make changes.

**Why "LISTEN UP" about change? Think employees would work harder if you took "change" out of their list of challenges? Think again. Change is the "breakfast of champions." When positive change is avoided, complacency takes over and failure is just around the corner. Read on!**

Change is tough. It's tough for all of us.

We often see you pulled between making a necessary change and dealing with our complaints and belly aching or choosing to avoid the change entirely. Sometimes it's simpler to keep the status quo. But, regardless how we act, we need changes to help us improve and we need you to confidently lead us though those changes.

In 500 BC, when Herclitus said, "The only constant is change," do you think he was talking about our company?

One of our peers once said that the only things that do not change are the vending machines in the lunchroom.

When you incorporate change within our team, you can count on the change — any change — being resisted. Change is as natural as breathing, yet most of us had rather take our last breath than make a change. Don't get defensive when we do not immediately accept what you are trying to change. Hang in there with us. The only way we are going to improve is with change, so regardless of how we may resist, we need you to lead us through the change process.

> Don't get defensive when we do not immediately accept what you are trying to change.

An old college professor once told us about a study conducted to understand how people react to change. Researchers took a mouse and four tubes, lying side by side on the floor. They put a cube of cheese in the second tube and released the mouse.

Off he went. When he scurried through the first tube and discovered it was empty, he quickly went to the second tube. There he found the cube of cheese, ate it and then went back home. The next day, he did the same thing. Soon he became conditioned, knowing there was no cheese in the first tube, and began going directly to the second tube to get his reward.

After several days, the scientists conducting the experiment moved the cheese from the second tube to the third tube. The mouse was released and, because of his prior conditioning, went directly to the second tube. But alas! It was empty.

So, what do you think he did? Go to the third tube, searching for the cheese? No. Did he go back home? No. Did he decide to go back to the first tube? No. Did he go back to the fourth tube? No. Instead, he stayed in the second tube, waiting for the cheese to appear.

He had become accustomed to finding the cheese in the second tube and when that changed, he did not — and could not — react to the change. If the scientists had allowed it, the poor mouse would have starved.

So, what's the point, you ask? First, when things change, let's not starve to death while we wait for things to go back the way they were (like the poor mouse). Our comfort zone becomes the greatest enemy to our potential.

Our comfort zone becomes the greatest enemy to our potential.

We're depending on you to attack complacency and not allow us to get so comfortable with the way things are that we cannot react to a change.

Secondly, the time to make change is when things are going well, not when we are starving to death. If the mouse in the experiment had been searching for more cheese while he was meeting his basic need of survival, he may have discovered a whole block of cheese in the third tube.

Change is more effective while things are going well. For instance, our sales people are much more effective

When things are going well, that's the best time for us to change — to grow, to improve.

prospecting when they have plenty of business coming in than when they don't. It's a strange concept that's really pretty easy to understand. When things are going well, it's time for us to change — to grow, to improve.

The chances of our team accepting change will improve in proportion to the trust you have earned, how much input we have in the change strategy, how much we understand about the change and the timing of it all.

Because we are all fallible human beings, we'll resist change to some degree, but we need your positive leadership to implement new ideas and to move us all toward improvement.

Speaking of positive leadership, we also need you to maintain a positive attitude even in times that may not be positive and are stressful for you. Your attitude has an incredible effect on the whole organization. When you are positive, we are more positive. When you are negative, we follow your lead. When you are stressed, we are stressed. We are a reflection of where you are and your attitude at the time.

People say that there are two enemies of optimism. One is worry and the other is negative emotion. We depend on you to lead the attack on these enemies and become a positive influence for the rest of us.

One of the group noticed that when you are worried about something, our whole team becomes paralyzed because of that worry. We become afraid of the uncertainty we feel and lose our focus on what we are trying to accomplish.

So, we are depending on you to stay focused on the result . . . we need you to keep your eyes on the goals we are trying to accomplish and look beyond the current and temporary trials we're facing.

> **We need you to keep your eyes on the goals we are trying to accomplish and look beyond the current and temporary trials we're facing.**

It is like when you arrive early at an action movie and walk in to see the last ten minutes of the movie. You see the hero and heroine riding off into the sunset and you know that, regardless of what happened before, everything ended happily ever after. Then, when you watch the movie from the beginning, your stress is less and you can even enjoy the perils facing the heroes.

It's much the same with your leadership. Keep us focused on the results you envision, even when the going gets tough. We need to know that the tough times we are going through are worth the trouble.

The majority of what you worry about never happens. Even if it the worst case scenario occurs, most of what you worry about is out of your control. Don't waste your energy on things that are beyond your control! When times are difficult, we want to help and if you involve us with the facts, we will help build a plan of action to make sure the worst doesn't happen.

One last comment about change and being an optimistic leader: Just like any other work-group, our team will have internal conflicts. When those conflicts arise, we are depending upon you to address the problem as soon as you see it happening. When our team is torn apart, nothing good is going to happen within our group. So, all we ask is that you get the facts, offer a reasonable solution and solve the problem right then. The longer a problem is allowed to exist within our team, the more energy it will take to solve. Address the problem now!

We all want to see things go smoothly — for you and for us. But, even when things are not so positive, we are depending on you to stay focused and to make something positive happen. Our team will be a reflection of your attitude!

# LISTEN UP!

## We want you to take a stand!

One of our highest priorities is to be loyal to you and our company. But, we will never allow you to earn that loyalty if you cannot be counted upon to have the courage to take a stand. While there will probably always be areas where we disagree, we should have enough respect for each other that we take the time to understand where each of us is coming from — and why.

Your courageous leadership can make a big difference in our success. We want you to have the courage to lead our team to grow, prosper and to become better at what we do!

[ 35 ]

Many people say the opposite of courage is cowardliness. Some say fear. While both have merit, we think the opposite of courage is conformity. Conformity means not having the guts to make decisions that will make us successful.

We are depending upon you to exhibit the courage it takes to clear the way for our success. If you want us to follow you, even in hard times, we need you to exhibit the following eight acts of courage:

1. **Have the courage to accept responsibility.** Yes, we've talked about this before, but if you are looking for excuses and someone to blame, we'll never get where we all are trying to go. Blame is looking to the past; responsibility is looking toward the future. We need you to accept responsibility and lead us to the future.

2. **Have the courage to seek the truth.** Things are not always as they seem. If you don't use all your resources to understand the real truth, you may make a bad decision. The higher you are on the organization chart, the more difficult it is to discover the truth. We are depending upon you to search for the truth and make adjustments based on facts, not perceptions or traditions.

3. **Have the courage to take risks.** Yes, we want you to take risks — as long as they are well thought out and the end result is worth the price we have to pay. In fact, we'll succeed faster if you will allow us to double our failure rate. Sound strange? You bet

it does.  But the more we fail, the closer we are to success.  A friend once said, "The definition of profit is a reward for risk." We want to profit

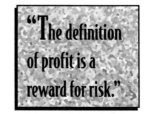

from our jobs, so we're depending on you to take the risks that are worthwhile.

4. **Have the courage to stand up for what you believe.** Most of us won't admit it, but we need a code of conduct to follow in our business lives.  Knowing what is acceptable and what is unacceptable under any circumstance eliminates stress. We also need to know corporate values and why those values should be important to us.

5. **Have the courage to reject the cynics.**  Hey, there are plenty of cynical people in our world – even in our company.  If you allow them to spread their cynicism, cynicism will eventually take over. We are depending on you to have the courage to address the cynics and take action to prevent them from destroying our team.

6. **Have the courage to give us freedom to be successful.**  We want to be the best in our jobs and at what we do.  We know it is hard to delegate and trust others to do something that you can accomplish yourself, but we need the opportunity to grow. If you do not allow us to learn, we will be at the same level two years from now that we are today. We need your courage to allow us to make mistakes — and grow from making those mistakes.

**7.  Have the courage to persevere.** The easiest path is to surrender, to give up. One of the keys to our success is to hang in there longer than everyone else. Don't give up on us or your vision of success. What separates winners from losers is the courage to hang in there long enough to win. We are depending on you. Never give up!

8.  **Have the courage to accept the responsibility for your role.** You are our leader and role model, everywhere you go and in everything you do. Don't waste your time asking the question, "Is anyone watching?" Just ask yourself, "What are they seeing and what direction am I leading?"

As our leader, you are an outstanding resource for us. You communicate to all levels of the organization. You help us find solutions to our problems and you create an atmosphere where we can all succeed in our work. Your role is important — enjoy it!

And we depend on you for so many things. We depend on you to maintain a sharp customer focus by building relationships with internal and external customers and to utilize every resource to improve overall customer satisfaction. We depend on you to help us achieve business objectives and to help us succeed, no matter how great the challenge. We depend on you to work within our code of conduct and to retain your personal and business integrity.

[ 38 ]

It takes courage to take a stand and accept the responsibility, as our leader. It takes courage to accept that everything you do counts. Just remember, the result of your courage is the influence that you have on us. Don't take that lightly.

# LISTEN UP!

## We want to work for the best!

**Why "LISTEN UP"** about people development? Today's employees like to work for the best and be a part of a winning team. When all is said and done, your job is to get results and in the process, develop your people. Read on!

We did not choose you to be our boss and you did not hire most of the people who are working for you now. But, regardless of how we all ended up on the same team, we have expectations of each other.

One of the expectations we have of you is to be the very best at the job you have chosen. We want you to grow and achieve so we will have an opportunity to grow and learn in our chosen profession.

We have all worked for many people in the past and we've discovered what separates the best leaders from the mediocre ones. It's the investment and commitment you

> **We're depending on you to know more than our competitors and we depend on you to push us to learn more than they do, too.**

make to learning and improving. We're depending on you to know more than our competitors and we depend on you to push us to learn more than they do, too.

Take time to learn! Just because you're a manager does not mean that your learning has peaked — or ended. In fact, you now are challenged to learn more rapidly so you can share that learning with others.

If you create an environment for learning, we will learn more and grow more skillful at what we do. Establish a library and we will read. Offer us audiotapes and we will listen. Go to seminars and send us to seminars and we will bring back good ideas to share with our team.

Teach us how to lead so that we will become more committed and begin preparing ourselves for the next step in our careers. Reward learning and we will be hungry to learn more.

Our last requirement is for you to enjoy your job and have balance in your life. You spend far too much time with us not to enjoy what you are doing. When you are happy, we are happy. When you are stressed, we are stressed. As we said before, you set the tone for the entire workplace. Don't take this responsibility lightly, but don't take yourself too seriously, either.

If you achieve all of your work goals and lose your family in the process, you are not the person we want to follow. If you abuse substances to help you cope with our challenges, you'll lose our respect and loyalty. If you are promoted three times in the next year and sacrifice your health, you are not the role model we want as a leader.

We want you to succeed as much as you want us to succeed — but not at all costs. We want you to be successful in all areas of your life – personally, physically, spiritually, and emotionally as well as professionally. Without this very important balance, you are not the person we want to follow because we will follow only the best.

> **W**e want to succeed as much as you want us to succeed – but not at all costs.

You have chosen to play a special role in our lives. We need each other to achieve our goals, both personally and professionally.

Our purpose in writing this book has been to contribute ideas that will improve morale, retention, loyalty and customer satisfaction. It is our sincere hope that you are now committed to LISTEN UP so we can all achieve extraordinary results!

## A FINAL THOUGHT

Leadership cannot be claimed like luggage at the airport. Leadership cannot be inherited, even though you may inherit a leadership position. There are no manufacturing plants that fabricate leadership and leadership cannot be given as a gift, even if you've been blessed with an abundance of leadership skills to share with someone else. Leadership is earned! It is earned by mastering a defined set of skills and working with others to achieve common goals.

Without question, the greatest leader of all time was Jesus Christ of Nazareth. In three years, He assembled and led a small group of dedicated followers who ultimately changed the world. He raised more capital than all other leaders in the past 2,000 years combined. His leadership philosophy was to do what was right, regardless of the consequences. He led with compassion, love, selflessness and understanding. We can learn much from His example.

May your journey as a leader bring success, balance to your life and increasing vision into the opportunities of the New Millennium.

# SPECIAL THANKS...

... to the following friends and customers who have provided us the opportunity to **LISTEN UP** and learn from their ideas and wisdom:

Ken Byrd

Ken Carnes

Phil Childress

Dr. David Cook

Paul Damoc

Bryan Dodge

Darryl Flood

Ed Foreman

Johnny Koons

Louis Krueger

Kevin Marshall

Bill McHale

Joe Miles

Fred Roach

Mark Shackelford

Tod Taylor

Bryan Tracy

Tony Van Roekel

Steve Weatherford

John Winkelman

And a very special thanks to

Mark Layton

for his creativity, encouragement,
and incredible vision.

# The CornerStone
# Principles of Leadership

## — VALUES PRINCIPLES —

1. The Principle of Integrity – Results improve in proportion to the level of trust earned by the leader.
2. The Principle of Responsibility – Results improve when leaders and their followers are held accountable for their actions.
3. The Principle of Commitment – Results improve to the extent that the leader hires and develops talented people.
4. The Principle of Vision - Results improve when leaders establish a crystal clear vision with a convincing reason to embrace the vision.

## — SYNERGY PRINCIPLES —

5. The Principle of Communication – Results improve when followers understand their role and are rewarded for their accomplishments.
6. The Principle of Conflict Resolution – Results improve when the leader timely removes obstacles inhibiting followers.
7. The Principle of Optimism – Results improve in proportion to the self-esteem and attitude of the leader.
8. The Principle of Change Management – Results improve to the extent that the leader embraces change and makes change positive.

9. The Principle of Empowerment – Results improve as followers are allowed to accept responsibility for their actions.
10. The Principle of Courage – Results improve in proportion to the leader's ability to confront issues affecting their followers.
11. The Principle of Example – Results improve when the leader is a positive role model.
12. The Principle of Preparation – Results improve to the extent leaders develop themselves and their followers.

*A full color*
*CornerStone Leadership Process poster*
*is available for $5.95.*
*Call 1-888-789-LEAD or visit*
*www.cornerstoneleadership.com*

**David Cottrell,** President and CEO of CornerStone Leadership, is an internationally known leadership consultant, seminar leader and speaker. His business experience includes senior management positions with Xerox and FedEx. He also led the successful turnaround of a chapter eleven company before founding CornerStone.

He is the author of *Birdies, Pars, and Bogies: Leadership Lessons from the Links* and *Leadership . . . Biblically Speaking: The Power of Principle-Based Leadership.*

He lives in DeSoto, Texas with his wife Karen and their children, Jennifer, Kimberly and Michael.

**Alice Adams** is an international columnist and speaker on communications, human relations and management. She is the author of two textbooks and currently heads Professional Resources International. Alice and her husband, Ron, reside in Austin, Texas.

# CornerStone Leadership Institute Offerings

## Leadership Development Training

### Building Your Leadership Foundation

One-, two- or three-day workshop designed to provide the front-line and mid-level leader the foundation for long term leadership success.

### Leadership, Biblically Speaking

A one- or two-day workshop connecting biblical principles to leadership in today's workplace.

### Leadership Lessons on the Links

A one-half day workshop teaching lessons on the golf course that can be applied in your business.

## Management Retreats and Keynotes

Call to book David Cottrell for your next management conference or keynote speech. His presentations have been popular at customer outings, golf banquets, leadership conferences, weekend retreats and staff meetings.

## Management Consulting

Winning begins with leadership and the CornerStone Leadership Institute will provide proven methods that get results for your business.

## Employee Surveys

Surveys customized to your specification that will evaluate the employee work climate within your organization.

## Books and Resources

*Birdies, Pars, & Bogies: Leadership Lessons from the Links* – A great gift for the golfing executive, golf tournaments and management retreats.
Paperback $12.95

*Leadership… Biblically Speaking: The Power of Principle–Based Leadership* – A guide on how to apply the leadership lessons from the Bible to today's leadership challenges. Hardcover $17.95

*The CornerStone Leadership Principles Process Chart* – A full color chart outlining the principles of leadership and the activities required to master those principles. $5.95

**For Additional Information
Call 1-888-789-LEAD or visit
www.cornerstoneleadership.com**

# Yes, please send me extra copies of
# *Listen Up, Leader!*

| Quantity | 1-99 | 100-999 | 1,000-4,999 | 5,000+ |
|---|---|---|---|---|
| Price Each | $7.95 | $6.95 | $5.95 | $5.50 |

**Listen Up, Leader!** _____ copies x $_____ = $_____

Shipping and Handling          $_____

Subtotal          $_____

Sales Tax (8.25% – **Texas Only**)    $_____

**Total** (U.S. Dollars Only)       $_____

**Handling Charges**

| Total $ Amount | Up to $99 | $100-$249 | $250-$1199 | $1200-$3000 | $3000+ |
|---|---|---|---|---|---|
| Charge | $6 | $12 | $25 | $65 | $100 |

Name_____ Job Title _____

Organization_____ Phone_____

Shipping Address_____ Fax_____

Billing Address_____ Email_____

City_____ State_____ Zip _____

☐ Please Invoice (Orders over $200) Purchase Order Number (if applicable) _____

Charge your order: ☐ MasterCard ☐ Visa ☐ American Express

Credit Card Number _____Exp. Date_____

Signature_____

☐ Check or Money Order enclosed payable to CornerStone Leadership
☐ I am interested in learning more about the CornerStone Leadership Process
☐ I am interested in having David Cottrell speak at a corporate/golf function.

**FAX**
972.274.2884

**Mail**
P.O. Box 764087
Dallas, Texas 75376

**Web**

www.cornerstoneleadership.com

**Phone**
888-789-LEAD